THE JUNTA OF HAPPENSTANCE

Tolu Oloruntoba

the JUNTA *of* HAPPENSTANCE

Palimpsest Press
1171 Eastlawn Ave.
Windsor, Ontario. N8S 3J1
www.palimpsestpress.ca

Book and cover design by Kate Hargreaves (CorusKate Design)
Cover photograph: "Warrior and Attendants" by the Edo people of the Benin Kingdom, on view at The Metropolitan Museum of Art
Author photograph by Franctal Studio
Edited by Jim Johnstone

A Anstruther Books

Palimpsest Press would like to thank the Canada Council for the Arts, and the Ontario Arts Council for their support of our publishing program. We also acknowledge the assistance of the Government of Ontario through the Ontario Book Publishing Tax Credit.

Canada Council for the Arts Conseil des Arts du Canada ONTARIO ARTS COUNCIL CONSEIL DES ARTS DE L'ONTARIO Ontario Ontario Media Development Corporation

Library and Archives Canada Cataloguing in Publication

Title: Junta of happenstance / Tolu Oloruntoba.
Names: Oloruntoba, Tolu, 1985- author.
Description: Poems.
Identifiers: Canadiana (print) 20210101539 | Canadiana (ebook) 20210101555 | ISBN 9781989287729 (softcover) | ISBN 9781989287736 (EPUB) | ISBN 9781989287743 (Kindle) | ISBN 9781989287750 (PDF)
Classification: LCC PS8629.L67 J86 2021 | DDC C811/.6—dc23

PRINTED AND BOUND IN CANADA

CONTENTS

I.

II.

III.

I

LOOKOUT

Your
one wing
-ed scapula: what does it mean?

Look out, child, clamber above
the fill line of the world:
if we are indeed part

of a continent and not alone,
where is everyone?
Our vise of hands

cannot hold counter-
clockwise flight,
is too confusing for radar:

this carceral island
will never keep us.
On an armspan

altar below
I imbue
the homespun

stone with a blue
animus,
a fletched offering

wind-ing you up.

EXPUNGE

Mantikore, they called the coffee thicket eating
the first sons of first sons to rise,
thorn incisors in a fugue face.

It has taken a whole saccharine country
and this runnel vision
to almost forget you.

That man-eater has been stealing
your gift of disquiet.

My coat is rafter guano,
beard a griot gyre as I shuffle,
dead-reckoning edges of your house;
I mimic the whitewashed walls,
I find the zodiac center
(or it finds me) where you, Taurus, lashed me red,
bound like the thief you thought I was.
Your bonds were good, lockjaw anklets
and bracelets. I counted to fifty
with my head, striking the ground.
This is why I can't remember.

UNDER THUNDER

Where does the ripping cord
of my unravelling wardrobe
catch and billow?

I consider tensile
strength as I hug my mother,
a little more slack
in my arms, my sister careening
from glassblowers, brightest
at her most brittle,
the sudden flare
of spirit before the break
of 40-Watt bulbs
under thunder.

The mediocre frost
of this aged winter
precipitates a memory
of drums in plastic lines,
throats expectant beneath
the asbestos rills: for rain
and decantation from corrugated
silt and worms that always
found the harvest.

How did I forget?
I consider semantic
search; I scour years

of vagrancy, the ten moves
of the last nine,
and scotomata, holes over my vision
of the Honda, laden with drinking kegs
as we sped from that decade.

MOOSE

Unless it's a moose,
you're better off driving through
the animal in your headlights
than swerving on the highway.
Of course, some choose to slow
like you do now,
coming from therapy
before the Gordian lurch
of some firm, then soft, speedbump.

MANTIS CORPS

The motherboard shorts, the mantis
corps, grown hungry, rub Stradivarius palms
for supper in downswoop, tooth
fillings strafe-gold, their swarm
a biblical maw with a cape of dusk,
a wake of dust, a bust of molten
rain. Their machine vision becomes actionable,
epaulet missiles speaking Hellfire.

If you disbelieve
the percussion of the field, what then
is this catholic appetite
of their edict, the bleached woodland they print
their beached whale font upon?
As above, terrible dactyls plunging to meet
the blood osmosis of the horizon, hesitating; so below:
your gunhand as *hors d'oeuvres*
for tyrannical Saurons. You obviously
have your own struggles. But perhaps
the beasts will want to share,
or kiss.

TINDERBOX

We were a conflagration asking
to be incarnated into the world.
Mother, superstitious, kept us
apart, two stones of the same
igneous anger.

Everyone saucered tears
like firetrucks before a plane crash,
as if preparing, should we combust.
Mother had once hidden
all the nooses, knocking
all hanging hooks from our ceiling,
the other family hid the tinder and wood,
crying flame-retardant
for the walls.

Your palm prints have returned
as shingles around my left eye.
There's extinguishing foam on the runway.
We meet again in our prefabricated peace.
Don't aim your will at me
if you will not shoot.

MEDICAL SÉANCES

Acolytes, we filed into a darkened temple,
luminous film of arcana below the false priest
at the lectern, casting visions overhead.
In the projection we learned to listen
for the murmurs of hearts that wanted to speak,
and the dead we did not allow to.

Pa James, he with the ligature of his hanging
still on, was our cadaver. We stripped the gnarly
windbreaker of his skin, his fleece of fat, for anatomy.
Routinely felled by formalin fumes at night,
it was worse later, in morbid anatomy, too-gleeful
residents brandishing sternal saws like breadknives.

All the dead could teach was the fear of life, and how
it can end. Benign sturgeons-general, schools in tow,
swam us past tufted-ear stingrays but we drowned still,
hydrophobic. Resuscitated after medicine, I remember
little but the Latin, an oculus being the grasp of a brain
on stalks. Pick your colour. Forgive me, father,

I am not the Esau you sought, with a stethoscope beard
to make you proud. Had I listened to spirits of dead
doctors who named everything after food—bread
-and-butter pericardiums, *café au lait* skin, *poma facies*
with nutmeg liver on a cribriform plate—
you might have liked the meal I made you.

AMPLITUDE

The Khoi-cracked earth,
a zipline,
a thoracic riptide;

the emptiness below my crab corset,
the need for more spine to consist
around, less war,

hard-er word: 'pacify,'
lithium law,
iron saw.

The first line
of wormcast
retracts me from the earth.

I find a word: 'adze,'
on the ground.
It is mine now.

You've heard said:
you shall not kill
in cities of refuge,

forming necklaced
avengers
of blood.

We remain
improbable
around this clatter

of smiles—
discussing death,
hacking after inner men.

A HISTORY OF TREACHERY

1851: The Bombardment of Lagos

Akitoye spoke to the witness cloud,
insidious then overwhelming
like the best bankruptcies.

The treaties promised all would be the same
as Gibbon's termite ate the stilt legs
of amphibious men who spoke Mammon.

Beware, we warned them too late,
the reverend caboceers,
the coastal commerce.

The enslavers will keep their maps
for when they reappear, righteous,
to civilize the heathens beyond;

and kingmakers who stack
vendettas from dust
must make their ramparts infallible.

The key to a large door
can be infinitely small;
a truce can be an iron foot in the gate;

all denudations must insinuate;
and the history of treaties
is still the history of treachery.

We hope only for benevolent conquistadors
who know the difference between
pretext and pretense,

and preventative protectorates,
bombardiers sympathetic
in their advance.

They had the best words (those British),
called it the Reduction of Lagos.
And in ten years, after the mortar ink had dried,

long before German civil engineers whited
fish bellies in the lagoon,
Queen Victoria was the King of Lagos.

1887: A Kidnap from Opobo

Jaja had grown Opobo into a palm
with oily fingers
that poked Liverpool's eyes.

Consuls roused the queen.
This crocodile user of juju
guarding her coveted Niger

never shut his eyes,
clenching estuaries by dance and stratagem,
his bulk and trade a dam on tributaries

with sluice doors of tax,
his backhand knuckled with war canoes
and 15 trading houses flocking his arbor,

his cannons trained up and downriver,
not amenable to glass bribes
and turns of phrase.

Importantly, he knew they fought
with paper and planted
cunning treaties of his own,

bottled and buried in fields at night
to root his feet in the earth.
When Europe scrambled from Berlin

to their slices of Africa,
they rushed again to snatch the oil river
with innocuous papers.

Sign here. [Undress first, this word, 'Protectorate,'
he said.] *We do not want your lands,*
only to protect them from the Germans.

Holding it against the light, he looked for the sting.
[But only if I keep my dams.]
They grew hungry again, frantic now.

Let this tree be ours. Or we cut it down.
(You may however board this gunboat to
negotiate another way.)

But having been enslaved in youth
[I'll die first] they dreamed up
another peace letter and sent it ashore.

But what is this seizure on deck
under the white flag of parlay,
the union jack unmoored,

inviting a sovereign in shackles to trial
in the marsupial pouch of night,
kidnapping for four years of tea

with the queen, if promised *free passage?*
Why did consuls say at once,
to Opobo, *Your king is exiled*

as they pumped jubilant puncheons
from the moat? They knew, didn't they?
A brutish contract

can be interpreted
however you wish
when you have machine guns.

1897: The Sacking of Benin

I am Ovoramwen, so I should know bronze
plaques are secretly brass, made of a wax
mold, a heat-proof core, shaped into story.

Melting the soft within, let dry
in polish for the royal rafters.
I cast this dirge plaque myself.

A half-millennium of wax was lost
in the siege, brass smelted
from the sentient manillas

smuggling treacherous spurs. Bini
has been anvilled by Maxim gun tracks.
into this tapestry of three bows:

the dirt in the mouth center;
abasing consul foot on the head stool;
chiefs who could not look, in suicide from the tree.

The guerrilla path I came to treat on
has been stunned by exhumed ivory
from my ransom grave.

Marine jackboots punished pride 1200 times,
a taxidermied republic of widows behind.
In relief, a lament of the breached earthen wall—

questions are omens striking hammers
from the plain. I am Ovoramwen,
so I should know to beware the British bearing

A Treaty of Trade and Friendship,
and that punitive expeditions are secretly
coups d'etat—chances to decant

my bronze into Brussels auctions
and London museums—another
ruby for Pax Brittania's gleaming

crown of blood. Hurrah for the Royal Niger Company.
Finish my plaque for me. Shine it. And set it
on this dust from which Benin has never risen.

HERETIC

The goats are breathing
shallower.

Listen
for the frog
tripwire, the cricket alarm
of footfall.

They will have doused
their lamps, but you can smell
the carbonaceous spirit
of raffia.

When they break
the crystal fence
of night with vaporous breath,
settle the mat;

and when they darken the lintel
with jute bonds

you're ready
for the forest.

HERETIC: TAKEN

Guardrails bay above
extraordinary renditions

of song under spotlight.
Which aria is yours in

the sodium sun
of interrogation,

from the prune belly
after an asker's tender

massage to help you
sing? Makeup: raccoon eye

gnawing sideways to cauliflower
ear; rehearsal: boxed

from the office at 4am:
an opera of grapnelled

wetsuits, an applause
of skylights

in the cymbal clash of pupils.
You speak so well,

surely you must sing, too?
To pianowire, *lente*,

electrode *molto allegros*?
Wake up. It's the crescendo.

Here comes your
redaction from the world.

ODE TO THE HELIX

The tannins have browned your double skin,
your cowhide robe, your velvet heart,
your handle, your pommel, the cruel knot
at the bottom good for long-range whipping.
Your two strands graceful, a denial,
a DNA of violence, your slender arms
foldable into switchblade elbows,
fetchable from the bottom drawer upstairs,
beside the thing stolen from me
for taking the thing that wasn't mine.

MANUBRIUM

I have lost the manubrium,
the mandible
of a laughing god
in bone fields,

Geiger counters
driven mad by radioaction.
Dreadlocks are icy grapnels I grasp in

journey to godhead.
My jacket grows heavy with
mushrooms on the journey up.

I am nothing
but a plexus of want,
mercurial residues couched in flesh,

and potions I've drunk daily for strength.
I rise unexploded, enriched, isotope-full.

After the mirage, I charge
backwards the long way,
black panzer over
fissile idols of my father

as the earth ticks with radium:
a borealis of seconds
undoing
the night as I work.

GROVE

In black light
the forest is an eyewhite fishbone grave—
we are bleached and all-pupil in its dark
and the curtains of the world
do not hush the dialtone traffic.

In black light
I asked for a diviner,
and one asked why I was sad.
I was,
when I looked.

You're molting, said another,
and I did,
when I looked.

SHE SAYS —

don't forget to breathe.
I grunt through
the bull run of my inner ribs,
my lungs a muslin sheath
of drum,
stagger off the panic bus,
pulled over, my night a drunk tank.

Here before my pill —
the fleet of plungers in my brain
ready to sail. Do we
need a prayer, or the like,
for this launch?

I've read the warnings:
this sertraline can reach
and slash your wrists.
But my dark foil is only
a suicide note
if it succeeds. Stop
when you find yourself
baying at the moon.

The elixir demands
scrapings from a sundial's millennial face,
from the skidmarks of its hours.

Autonomy texts show my skull sliced
open after, for ventilation.

The brain has no nerves of its own
so I feel none
of the disrobed ants, their clothes
crackling with light. They wear
only boots of dry ice and pneumatic drills.

Their mother is the wedding of depth
gauges, diviner, a wrecking ball of lie-detector eyes
and jawbones.
I want her to reveal
the secret of blood,
how saplings questionmark
the morning above ground.

She says—

A FINGER IN THE EYE SHOULD DO IT

The doc explains the hole in my brain
with a purgatory of plastic poppies:
a glom, a vortex of exit wounds falling out.

Planets of fruit wax and their storm drains,
a Dreamliner of swordsmen falls out.
Cesium-blind drone boys, and their Elephant Foot

fall out. Housing bubbles, unexpected contraceptive,
the cower and triumph of the inadvertent falconer
fall out. Train cars, in white-cane folds fall out.

Mother, riding a Shel Silverstein allegory falls out.
The monomania of ferry conductors,
their anchors of nose rings, their barnacle hooks fall out.

Grey matter in peristaltic ropes,
a bucket of neurotransmitters,
an expanding slick of blood falls out.

If the mask of the maw be grotesque,
how much more what is beneath?
What if the accordion of breath be broken?

What of the resonance of bridge boots
breaking the boombox first?
I don't know, but it seems a bit much, doesn't it?

Knowing if, or that I've died? Will you help me look?

WE WILL HAVE QUESTIONS

We will have questions about this in the morning.
I present my skull as exhibit:
observe the nuclear shadows inside,
flat-ground molars in devil's grin.
What medallion was this for?

Lonely brewmasters nurse an antediluvian
premonition for the world.
If we are eating as friends can we
swap stories over the cauldron?
There's a brave figurine in there
bobbing to the surface of a second drown,
treading soup
for morning or the succor of spectators.
The soldier-base of his feet
is the pocketwatch of long campaigns.

Not unlike birds, many before us have
taken wirecutters to their feet, to
reverse-crash from the slop,
seaplane-churning their arms for flight.
I can tell you therefore at last—I
am upright only because
if I ever lay down a minute, I may never rise.
Quitters, who can neither shut their eyes tight nor
open them wide,
know to tamp the fission
of unravelling thought till the end.
We'll come to the finer points of escape
but tell me again, why you made this war?

PATRIMONIAL

sabotage:
the best bomb closets
for therapy sappers

to lose their limbs.
Sacrifice: demography
for a despot, papier-mâché god—

demon graphite, daubed graphic,
marking census
from carpal tunnels.

You can choose your weapons upstairs:
argumentative sabres, fog-lit rapiers,
arachnid traps,

but my worship
at this table
is done.

You'll come down,
I sense,
in your own time.

II

CHILD AT SLEEP

Swan necks knuckle the jamb,
the safecracker ear,
and buckle of spine.
Soon, the listener sieves
the distant sound of breathing.
Pattern birds carry
proof of life in currents through
the wallpapered wood:
within the accordion crib
the machinery of rib walls
crates air for the world.

CO-EXIST

Africans never presume to count another's children,
so we don't know how many they had, the family
ours moved in with, each sidestepping the other.
Mostly. Avoidance was respect: night was their time,
the musical clan tapdancing ceiling boards to pipes,
and winching squeaks from plumbing, chorus stars
above, cosmic dust, pointilist, in sifted asbestos below.
You would go into their kitchen at night for water
and see their conspiracy scattering, snooker balls
struck by light, darting stragglers huffing for the pocket
hole. Easy, having nibbled their doors under ours,
thoroughfare through the house and gourmet gougings
of bread, each mousehole ornate. Losing their shyness,
we occasionally met at dusk, their whiskers tightrope
lances measuring the abyss of air on either side,
sifting our intention, teaching the resonance of mice:
while the world continues to build ours at the edge,
to wrench our microcosm from potential space.

INCURSUS

Happening on the fence of Eden,
night resolves into griffin guards
we had not seen, matte against
the confluence beyond, iron
shavings of pupils
shoved apart by what light there is.
Toil, toil, toil, they chant with
the night in angelus, lance butts on the mulch.

The adaptation of gloom's creatures:
firefly points of a spiked scarab, also a plough,
in the chromatography of denial,
in the assured prevalence of gravity,
and as happens, always in paradise,
the incurse beyond it,
the gangrene from tourniquet,
the ancient curse, *toil, toil, toil*
rippling concussive from the center.

Grant audience, or armor from your world, I pray.
Job was a better man than I.
Don't try to take my child.
I beg.

PATTERN RECOGNITION

From the crash of the Paleolithic
on concentric days
it's a circular route,
a roving dome of dark.

The companion of moments
ago will dissolve,
become a carousel of arms,
a whir of charcoal into black

and I a coat hanger of pleas,
boxing the envelope
of blindness. Approaching
the other rotor in my space,

the thrum of electrostatic
greeting startles,
the memory of voltage attracts,
the friction of sensate digs spurs the canter,

collection of charge for later
experiments, calibrations through
chest walls, of hooves bearing
a mute, unravelling eureka, harried,

hurrying. In the half-decade of nighttime
necessities there's a suggestion of warmth,
a rumor of contained dawn below,
a sputter for us to invent fire.

MANGONEL V. EXOCRAFT

Who's the
homunculus with the trigger?
It has my beret on.
For eyes: a 6face die, an 8ball,
its slotmachine heart running on
probability
that the house always wins.

I'm hit.
What's this sigil of unfurling stains,
the sternal moth on my cyborg plate, the bloody mouth?

What's that proxy struggler,
spine of compact discs slipping in
the martial music
of the fall backward,
Chekhov's
Gatling
raking the sky?

On ground, ants unbraid my hair
for the callosal mainframe
and the computations of phrase within.
Deliver me from amputation.
Blink if you hear me.

FEUD(AL)

1.

If the timeline ahead is
infinitely longer than the
knives behind, perhaps
as we set to mending
we can heal more
than we ever undid.

But we, too,
would like a piece of the plunder
or have the bank to buy it,
a piece to hold
risen, lords of stolen land, washed
in the blood
of the deed.

2.

I pull my broadsword umbrella
from its sleeve
and charge through the acid rain.

3.

Composition:
lidless or closed
circuit eyes; nipples
profuse, the hydrant rash;
tail-lit lice leaving
blood tracks;
the night light
cloak, the belly-up animal,
the phallic spires,
stretchmarks
tracing navel
to suburbia,
belly growls
of traincars
as I stand by
the marsupium and jump.

4.

Dark, I raise you an intractable struggle.
Sky, bear witness. Face down
on the massage pillow
of this valley, I know you see.
By the Air Jordan
scar on my chin,
bald as his head,
by my Excalibur grip
of the train bars,
two-handed,
if the cars of this SkyTrain were to skid off centrifugal,
whiskered by hydraulic tendons,
accordion-folding for the river
as death reaches a watery spike for my heart,
I wouldn't die.
I have paused to ask how, or why, I wouldn't die.
Why I want to survive, or why I will,
car top shorn,
extending my sword-arm
to you from the lake.

5.

What to do if I die:
before I set, form my lips into the final syllable
of what I've been trying to say,
a snarl before smelting in the crematorium.
Shorn of oxides, can ashes make an ink?
                                        Print that.
The folder is named "I will not die," but of course, I did.

HAS ANYONE STUDIED THIS?

The darker pixels of the piechart slice
each find it too hard to continue,
and consider immolating themselves.
Call it statistics, the sludge drifting off
tectonic page. The standing committees
of traincars tells me this is true:
the communion of misery;
commiseration, microdosed migration.

I keep hoping for the rockslide of books,
the horology of logs in a turn of phrase
at the vertex of impact,
to boost something in me.
Is anyone threading our empty heads?
If you did, you might see this is getting worse.

IF, GOATHERDS

this path is blind with rocks,
can we try the trusted
feint, the lane
with vines twined
in an afterglow of sun?

Stunned on spaghetti paths, heartblood still
on my guilty staff, I cannot say I'm good.
Eagle lime grows the mountain yearly.
We could tap the telltale thud,
following the vein, the lightening seam
but now,
on each shard
of us
is coal
to blow
for joy.
The goats will be fine,
or not.

No matter.

OPTIC CHIASM

If you care, the roof of your nose is a nerve sheaf,
an intersection, half of each eye's record crossing
the junction, slithering for the back room, taped
into what you see. *So what?*
If your eye causes you to sin, the book says,
grind it into birdseed, let your carddeck brain
swap that feed with black, a blanket over the field.
So what? If your eye is lazy, should it eat?
If your eye is a stained window of inner chambers;
if you find you can't calibrate the right amount of sleep
to dislodge the anvils of your lids and chest;
if your islets, lacing a diligent atoll falter
into an inlet for rays of the world, say, of a test blast;
if you say your expectations are managed,
you want only to make it from bed daily,
and your inner I, unguarded, catches an afterimage
of that unhappiness, a spectral self limp in its jaws,
so what? Flashblindness. You only die
if you see the white phosphorous of its glare.
Otherwise—keep going.

VIA NEGATIVA

A 15-year abacus, a rosary of flint faces,
and an inverted road.
Jonah, personal patron, pray for me.
You brother of cowards and fugitives,
welldigger who struck a bedrock
of scorpions every time.

I too have encountered
a rising tide of what could be water,
if it wasn't paralyzing me from the feet up.
It's that venom for the black market,
the good stuff I move in lucrative spreadsheets.

I suspect I have no idea what I'm doing,
and these detours may kill me,
but if I cross off every wrong road,
my tally may pave a final one for me.

PLEASE STAND CLEAR OF THE DOORS

Outside, surveillance turrets hang like
reverse Gatling guns scooping the photons
we scatter in morning rush.

An infrared dot plot would show our swarm,
bleeding in pulses, from valvular doors.
Even security camera clerks hate their jobs,

so what would it take for this arbitrary economy
to block an artery and die?
After the aura of a well-timed seizure we carry

OLED lights in solemn march, and fire up the anthill
of anthills together,
carrying a dome of light into downtown dawn.

SIEVE

Why am I still so insulted by visa lotteries
that sift migrants—I, in particular?

Do I think I'm above the seed hopper,
the jostle to be one of the good ones?

The amulet of meritocracy has failed, obviously.
This is the junta of happenstance.

I could return to the tracing of despair
my country has become,

or adopt the patience of the indentured,
the grit of the gambler:
two more years, and then we rest.

HIRED HANDS

By the adz and blackpowder,
and the migrant hands to hold them
in charge through the mountain;

by locomotive strikes of mattock on rock,
powered by the carbon of pressurized bodies;
by the strata of laborers waiting to become

clean coal, as we call it now,
holding up a conceptual America,
artisans of shovel, and barrow, and keyboard;

we have laid the tracks,
been bayonet for the gutting hand trundling down them,
tip of the spike stirring the ozone, growing still.

SETTLERS' EFFECTS

Do you ever know if a country is yours?
Through heavy-lidded skies, and crop-dust lines,
hellish staircases water the horizon.

Mileage expands westward:
bugs sheen the windshield,
roadside, raccoons stick in backstroke,
and the waterless urinals of rest stations
have the nail-white bowls that will save the planet.

Derricks and horses graze
the mass grave of North America,
brochures instructing us to enjoy the desperate
beauty of its desktop wallpaper:
mountains, farms above,
oil below, torque in F-150 gear shifts—
speed, times inertia, to the power of error.

Convenience stores in Mountain Time
save scowls of the old west for strangers.
It's a little boring; the Stephen King towns are all alike.
I don't know how these ones will end,
but we've seen *Poltergeist*.

All our goods as tribute for the one Crane Operator,
with invisible market hand, and scaffolds of cored blood,
cement from the bone powder of endless conquest,
fit for an endless tower,
an international space station at the top.

AD79

The Vesuvius horse—
a gelding, obviously—
harnessed still and petrified
these 1940 years,
is saddled for the ride
the masters never made
to the mountains.
All that grooming and shoeing,
to be bound still, even in death.

Archaeologists will find us
encased, one in tent city
tarp, the other half
in Styrofoam, chained
to phone cable and extension cord,
winning the penultimate round,
but losing the last together,
obviously, as old stars
and new satellites bear witness

to our time-lapse:
glowing, whisking, gone already.

III

THE CREATION OF MAN

There, amidst the dry faucets of water cycles, the ketones of God's breath pricked my nostrils, stunned as I was after the birth canal, and I became a living soul.

From that vapor nanites, industrious, had gone to my washing cylinder core, and set it to spinning. There's the secret of perpetual motion we've failed to replicate: to pass the torque to progeny and, worn, be swapped out, world without end.

Perhaps that's why I don't dwell on those first seven days, or trillion years, and ask nothing for myself anymore.

And so my gravitational whorl drew me to metallic feet while my parents lay, serpentine in a sleep they made. A zygote knows something, or nothing, of violence, but I'm told there had been a miscarried world before this, flushed in a deluge of red.

And God said: let's try this again.

CONTINENTAL WANT

Ayò is our two-lane mancala:
remove seeds, count seeds, plant,
capture children of a Black Atlantic.

We are the boarding pass pre-break:
ambitious / amphibious on either side,
manacled to exile,
the random rulership of chance and
the tartan memory of chain-link fences,
our office coffeepot black
with offshore labor in the morning.

If Ayọ̀ is joy, then we wish:
Ayọ̀ á kárí, that the brownthumb of travel
be unable to wilt us;
for the roulette of passport control
to dispense enough joy
into alm-bowl hands,
ballast to ford the oaths
they put all we wanted behind.

CHAW

I grow in the wrong places

for gnawing
the incisors of my upper jaw keep growing

I sharpen them on others

I disappear myself, sabretooth man
into caves

dissolving into the
archaeology of the world

anatomy of a non-accidental injury

by the handle and keyhole
of my breastbone
open me

like you would a chest

part the pulleys   of my neck
and pericardial drum
please

how diminished do I return?

what does it say?
does my arc portend
a salvation?

MY THERAPIST ASSESSES SUICIDAL IDEATION

My own stigmata are different:
I never return calls, another way of cutting
myself from the mind of the world.

I go to my
carnivorous plants out back:
trigger plants, with velcro pantsuits of death, clutch
    stomachs;
powdery strap airplants and guiding pilot lights,
to sticky strips for the unknowing;
pitcher plants and pitcher-trap ambushes awaiting
    the totter,
the topple, the drown in digestive drums;
twining bladderworts and purple, delicious, dervish skirts;
venus flytraps belching beyond tripwires and the
    clap of cymbal doors;
waterwheel plants, whorls of snap-traps sieving,
    wading the water,
washing me down;
Sundews, anyone, anemone home for a warm shower?
Here, midges around a touchscreen moon, I can slurp
the capsized roof
of the pond.

My mind has bent the facts, I know.
The facts have bent my mind.

CHUCK NORRIS

We have so much to blame Chuck Norris
for, circumcising villains
with bullet-hot bayonets in flick after flick,
headband soaked with righteous facepaint,
dispatching baddies with dance:

the Tarantella, the shimmy and shake
of exit wounds in time to clattering clips,
casing mountains swelling under conjurer hands.
Helicopters rise above the grounded sun
of napalm villagers and, again, that dance

under disco ball grenades, on the muzzle-flash,
rocket-red stage as America prevails.
America always arrives in time to save
those who have waited, faithful;
those who have whetted their eyes

on window slats; who have survived,
unwilted, the air raids. Your brave,
your bandana-partial, bring them.
Chuck, with two priapic carbines will
slo-mo run back for you. And so we went.

WHEN MIGRANTS GATHER TO ENJOY

the plunder that preceded us,
the eyelets, fishhooks of the dead
try to snag our glances;
so
much
blood swamps here that those
who perceive it drown instantly.

When migrants gather, they do not
enjoy their arrival. The land
is diminished up close
and everyone
wants
theirs
before it's gone. We are not
responsible, we say,

for the strip-mining of others,
eyes shut behind the flag slats,
faces plaster-stripped
with the eclipsing light
of city-
building;
we were hired only to truss
these drill towers on arrival.

3D printers make more of us
to erase everything—
quick soil for group graves,
and the marchers
propping
the door.
Blood everywhere.
We buy more boots.

IN WHICH I, AGAIN, AM FIGHTING MY WAY OUT OF THINGS

Submerged into words on the bus, I sink,
lances of spring light fenestrating
the darkroom of my eye. All
the buses of this route
are fused into multiverse,
mitochondrial microcosm
on the miniature Pennsylvania Rail.
One of these things is not like
the others: it hyperventilates
for a dive into macadam,
sending sonar for the blowhole
of this town. I can tell you now—
my oath was always hypocritical—
I only wanted exit keys for that citadel,
a Heracles butterknifing my way out
of the trash disposal belly
of filial duty, rotor teeth tapering
into ribbons of lead. On ground,
I let the light of a cheeto sun raise
my serotonin, seek lift from the thumb,
the teat of helium tanks,
concentrators of lower density,
and await my summons,
the splintered instructions I must write.

GREEN / HOUSE

1.

Green house in-finite, mirror of the despoiled world,
roiling flame of blue diagnosis;
expeditions, for God beyond dictionary precipice,
the box canyon of perdition. Heading home
to original chaos, pops
of a craft directed to supper, my body
jointed by welding, mouthguard soup telling,

al dente tongue sweet. Next the whisked
contrails of flagellating comets, face-
tious hurl of stone fruit, molten cores, to perihelion.
First dying in post-prandial tide,
what new name from tomb, from which other names?
Penance, existential sacrament of apostate geometers.
You flicker in zebra rind dermatomes,

concrete flesh halted in rigorous tasks.
Try the carapace flay for the nanite of faith.
These really are the bandages of death,
with slots for coins, two for eyes, and one for toll:
the disc battery of your breast bone. All this to say:
from your sprawl, we start the old dig again.
Speak. Present your wakened questions and symptoms.

2. Àkúdàáyà

I, West African, am rightly superstitious of pawpaws,
their secrets like flintlock seeds; and the dead
returned before we know their labor has ceased,
when they can't resist a final glimpse, rays
of those they need after they die out of town.
They're back to better, slower, second life,
if we can call it that, hiding from the Reaper's rage.

They sip, they kiss, linger longer, more studious:
gone is the primal impatience. I imagine B,
secretly dead these 15 years, and my double-
take at his sister's, my aunt's, house.
What are you doing here? Found out, he instantly
dissolves. Worse,I won't be able to blame him.
How many have been allowed to love,

then allowed to leave friends at the doorway?
Who would choose that, if they could?
Fine, I'm a little old for ghost stories.
The passing, the past thermohaline currents:
the sweat and warmth of everyone alive
are the strings of their show, compelling
confrontations here. Death might be just a passageway.

I, coward

curl away still,

but an end may merely reprieve from the wounded earth.
Let it take you, zipline from the treetops.
Embrace the hoist. Perhaps the door is thus, no step
onto emptiness from a bad day. Trust the harness,
the basket, the carriage return, the next line of the heart.

3.

We'll even take that weakest of plot devices—
a *deus ex* for the lonely. The chyron, garrote
of radio waves, the new neck brace of fingers,
the flex begun again. What are we to do
on the coming plain and as for mission,
can it be lost in marionette noise, heedless
Marie Antoinettes chuting like serial trees?

We strain for the peculiar note of home, our chorus
keening, crying in Eden fall, rent from the Voice
like, before us, all others. Fists of solo flight—
the aerodynamic lines of descent smelt you into the air-
grasping hand, suction the wrist,
body the mother—gravity. In your depression,
paleontology shows we crash, always alone,

in an amniotic craft glinting the day off:
igneous Daguerreotype, probing head set
in Edvard Munch scream. I know what is against me:
I am not brave / enough, cannot hear, sometimes.
Speak, Lord. Death lurks in mangrove-clasp
against the stem of life, against my scarab,
my mustard seed husk, my origami cosmos within.
    Whenever

the water scents me let me   unfurl from earth
    in farewell.

OUR LADY OF DELIVERY EXCELLENCE

Coffeepot communion.

Do this in memory: the kitchenette waltz, line up to
  receive the host.

We need new ambitions,
to be made soapleaf
from lays with other lyes,

to lap the grave, soup from froth, lie before the host.
Call us fardel,

for we are exact, calculated beneath the number of
  alarms needed, crowded round escapes too narrow
  for our stamp from these stacks.
Fire codes demand a good burn,

productivity in these factories, conference calls as
  somniloquys, cinquain, tetralogy, triptych and duet,
  solo, die before the host.

Wine before the host.
We're either unwashed or too
white, and neither will matter
when she arrives
to purge the chosen.

Pass the chalice.

BLOODLETTING

The theory of in-flow and out-go
made physicians of old
bloody indeed.
Whatever went in to ail
must be brought out again—exorcising
lance and blade, leech and purge,
plumbers bleeding valves off two millennia
of sick. How else to deal with poison?

This is what homeopathic deans,
saints and charlatans knew
of poetry,
why we drink diluents,
potent books to wash us out,
poured through activated charcoal
pencils filtered again in paroxysmal
dialysis twice a week.

At sedentary workstation, things pool
decubitus toward my bottom
and I must descant them
before they make me mad. Crab-like,
I scrabble abracadabras on my desk
to disappear into the caffeinated pools
spurting from my wrists.
How else to deal with poison?

Later the antidote, first the purge.

GAMBIT / SALVATOR

The bronze Bonaventure Christ
has a parka of snow
on his shoulder today.
Against the 8am, long suffering
shadow, the gladiolus
of his outstretch interrupts
the lawn. I don't know, Christ,
should I interrupt this bus?

REPAIR

Ice universes of your awl awaken me
to your train of your thought,
archetypes, pre-loaded motifs of man
after Auschwitz, and our new knowledge of him.

The dress of evening billows in
the blow of blue round your chewed
bone of moon. Your made world.
What shock from calm entry

into the poet cauldron of stasis
and moving stone, moss lording the cracks,
droplets clinging to the petal cliffs.
Risk a closer vantage, bluff overlooking

the house with windowed mage
naked of surrounding scape,
lone in a plane of glass, typewriter
ribbons fissuring its globe. That shoe

has no need for satyrs of the dream,
in the forge, from the cup to the cast,
the lost wax of your bronze crouch
reveals only you, foil in the space below.

Is it any wonder you survived the tantrum
of passing if you resurrected a mother,
lover and hare not soul only, but flesh almost?
In the depths of your hardback trapdoor

is an expanding cosmos, a tree alive
with ants and their pirate armada,
their king commanding the tankering of ichor,
a King Owen: seven days fetching your blood

and sprinkling it, gas ascending the satiated
earth. Last things, death masks have no use
for the living. You show the lie,
torture chamber of self, nail in thalamus,

sledge we inflict no more. The canal
skeleton of the dark calling attention to itself,
and the dance of woof woods, and weft winds
darning after biopsy extracts a loathing

from the breast. You are the island in cosmic globe
where you never die, whence from dirt
the flurry of the song, awakened, of your swifts:
after kindness to yourself, having tried so hard,

perhaps an invisible mending follows.

BALLROOM

Begin always with Ondine's Curse:
aflutter a few moments till we forget
to breathe. Then the myoclonus—
bowel-snatch of gravity,
the knee jerk, twirl at sleep edge
feinting two-step with spectral other:
umbra, penumbra, again.
You need all the things that begin
to fail you: firm knees, a memory
of steps, and the equanimous
smirk of mastery. *Homo terraformis*—
inventive arbiter, meet the poly-thumb
of time, anvil of a risen twilight,
the osmium apron, its shadow fence.
In vain you line your cracks
with a lotion armature, praying
to lightning for a current to unpack
your eyebags, to will backward
the treasonous body, its orchestra
winning in tripwire trills,
airhorn sections, snare tremolos
of imploding nailguns
percussing the hardwood floor.
Still, wrought iron shoes can wrest
only the next footdrop from the fog
machine. Picking through littered
organs ruins our rhythmic trawl.
Why protect the shoes?
It's a fine night on the floor.

IV

EMERGING

As if to harvest sweetness from me
bees of the gable
grab my head in exit,
the laugh tracks of sudden rain
timing my stilted rise: radicle,
my lengthening question mark; plumule,
periscope for a light that must be; cotyledons
flailing the bronze death of embryonic sleep
and roots tapping the hum of earth
through the soil, the thorny hands reaching
for my erupting head, my flower

crown. I've been seed, singular, false
eye of peninsula, storm-lashed, shorn by
nutcracker teeth of a shore entry.
But if the altar of flotsam holds as staircase,
as lighthouse, I will be saved.

WHY WE DIE

Allegorical comets
trace parabolae
to Orion's buckle,
our taillight from the void;

infirm treads
down bean-
stalk beltholes
of shrinkage,
and loanshark grips
of bladder necks,
and allegro rattles
of beleaguered lungs

launch pleas
at me, but my grievances
aren't doing this. I'd give
leave, could I grant it, but I don't know
why we die.

IN FETU

Here's the city, dying twin, papyraceus
siphoned from navel siege ramps,
neighbors smuggling petrol
out of the country and Kalashnikovs in.

Here, I, anointed, teach preformation—
from miniature homunculi
we sprout, premade in costly condominiums,
grown like Lugard's bad seed.

I deliver mothers of their children,
sending Leopold maneuvers
to warn them of this place. It is
their partners that are hysterical, gripping

my shirt collar, their migrant uteri
roughing me up. Sympathetic pregnancy
we call it. And yes, I'm aware of the absurd
history of hysterics and obstetrics.

Perpetually *in fetu*, midwives ride
the mountain of my mother in vain.
The cut under is fluvial, a Y-confederacy,
disbanded. I bustle to bind the infirm

with mortar dust, who want me to bind
faster, who must never know my work
is not science yet. We have re-turned
to dark arts: burial-shroud children

guarding the perimeter. They bivouac
in the charnel barracks; they lob
their fast-forward wilt into domes above us.
My guild is fled. Succor me, winch me now.

MEDICINE

It was only ever about my own patient
excision, incision, tunnels as train
religion, hugging the walls in oncoming
shake, flattening in the perpendicular
congress of tracks, the points of spaced
insults, at speed, coalescing
into the becoming: man of faith,
here's a man of doubt.

Opening crawl:

lightning chalks a descending cumulonimbus.
Dramatis persona: we know the prime
as he enters the frame, his foreshadow
a skin of death, a long hood. But if the canary-
down torch lights in this funk,
he'll be golden. Drained in hot morgues,
the substance of mind is harder still

than the soft sheath of belief, scarified
with a swaddling of inky inoculation:
hamsa, haibun, halter hitch, ampersand, hymn.
Febrile, I leach sweat into the mattress,
takeoff maimed. But, doubtful apostle,
there is some breath left to me. And if anyone
could find me in a valley of ribcages,

you could.

Strap me to your cart.

Run me, if you can, from the city.

VINCULUM

The urge to whittle is all that's left of these experiments:
insular activity in an avalanche of conifer cursors,

amputations, trepanning for the manifest destiny
of my thoughts to yeast over; a lighted wick for my ear,

and if rope burns do not consume the belt, I will be held.
Where has all conviction gone? Chisel it down,

that exo-body, for truth: if there's hope for a greenstick
slashed, scenting water, my spiral-cut femur

in periosteum sling, will await rumors of blood.
The harness, marked with the end of lexicons

is broken. I am thus given to divination,
casting lots for coordinates of origin to reverse

my Samarkand from sand. I lost my fight
with God but ask, at least, safety from the arena.

IF TILDES APPROXIMATE WINGS FOR THE BARREL I'M IN

If sweat from my rambling
makes a moat after
the invitation of windowpane sparrows
to jump,
I will be saved.

If a tilde and twin approximate wings ~O~ for the
 barrel I'm in,
if the tattoo of feet becomes serpent black on a
 songbook lattice,
if the bunched fingers in a barbed fence are pruned
 into epileptic
runes in a vèvè of blood, I will be saved.

I will be saved I
will be saved say
the word I will be saved.

The maneuvers of Leopold's amputees, querying a
 pregnant sky
are practice, too;
the coaxing of sap quick enough,
palms cupping
a Belgian bowl is prayer, too;

and fasciculations of wrist muscles, timing the echolalia
of ask
are clapping, too. And if in the grocery store of
bewilderment,
I can stock my basket with oil, if I am an adobe hut,
matchstick-red,
and the dissident strikes the walls within,

bending terra-cotta
knees
before the light,

if the gauntlet of space junk
round the planet reflects, repeats
my immolation
to me in an offset twinkle of smelt,
ashes, to dust, to glass eye,
Zeiss ball, if I can still see then, even dim, I will be saved.

SPARUS

This neural mesh, the coral brain of sads knows
when another of us is sunk. Some speak of Grey Goo,
the mitotic mush that will eat the world.
It already has, and the sertraline suds of our sewers
have not washed away
the denticulate scum, the flocculant armor,
the rafted pleas of the river for blood.

Sentence the hanging trees, too, to death, then.
It is only right to pulp their flesh, and char the inked scroll.
It is only right to trace the unravelling of silicon,
rappelling up the beach,
wicking an in-finite apron line.

Settle the shelf, then, let's. The reef
calls our skeletons as symbiote schools nibble
them clean. *Human bones*
make for terrific daggers. Cast off the land,
our accreting forest, limestone spears, our stalagmite lunges,
our congress can pierce   the belly
of a continent.

LIFE BY A THOUSAND BANDAGES

After the thousand cuts,
the one death,
comes the thousand bandages.

As we repair the house of annealing
from that primordial mound of plasters,
a spark.

Within I'm more darn than breach,
an eruption of stitches,
an avalanche of thimbles as sweat.

If my bandages be an armature,
and the balm a lighter fluid in wait,
then from the inevitable weight, a combustion comes,

a stirring, a galactic implosion of cosmic night,
cowering elbows flung in the shrapnel of a saving bang.
I will come forth.

ACKNOWLEDGEMENTS

I respectfully acknowledge that this book was written on the ancestral homelands of Iroqouis and Lenape people in what is known today as Pittsburgh, Pennsylvania (Dionde:gâ'); and Surrey and Vancouver in British Columbia, on the territories of the Semiahmoo, Katzie and Kwantlen, xʷməθkʷəy̓əm (Musqueam), Skwxwú7mesh (Squamish), and səl̓ilwətaʔɬ (Tsleil-Waututh) Nations. I am committed to justice and restitution for them.

In writing these acknowledgements, I realized that the book I began with, including many of the poems I wrote in my first sixteen years of writing, had been snake-sloughed in favor of poems I wrote in the 3 years that followed. A book wants what it wants, and the junta of this book decreed what to include. I therefore have two books' worth of thanks to give, and apologize in advance for how long this will be. All errors and shortcomings remain mine.

Jim Johnstone, when I was only a few months into my stay in this country, selected my chapbook *Manubrium* (in which some of the poems in this collection appear), for publication by Anstruther Press. It was a miraculous, almost mystical, turn of events because his collection, *The Chemical Life*, had showed me that what I was trying to achieve with my poetry was possible. I fashioned *The Junta of Happenstance* with that inspiration, and that permission. What a boon it has been to experience Jim's kind and perceptive counsel, wisdom and decisive guidance, and the panoramic-yet-detailed editing that made this book what it became, and brought it to you.

My sincere thanks go to Aimée Parent Dunn, publisher of Palimpsest Press, for taking a chance on this book and giving it a home. I hope that your faith is rewarded. Daniel Scott Tysdal discerned the early shape of several of these poems, and his keen editorial eye produced the best debut chapbook I could have ever hoped for. I thank Victor Ehikhamenor and Osemhen Okenyi for their advice regarding the choice of cover image for this edition. I thank Kate Hargreaves, who was responsible for the stunning design of this book, for bringing it to life.

Shazia Hafiz Ramji's kindness has meant the world to this serial immigrant. Thank you for welcoming me, first, into Canadian letters. In that home, I have been blessed by the comradeship and generosity of Aidan Chafe, Canisia Lubrin, David Ly, Dina Del Bucchia, Sean Cranbury, Kevin Spenst, Hasan Namir, RC Weslowski, Shane Neilson, Ian Williams, Fiona Tinwei Lam, and Dionne Brand. I would also be nothing as a writer, and person, without the life-giving friendship (and beta reading) of Olukemi Lawani, Jide Adeyefa, Namrata Singh, David Olamide Craig, and Abayomi Ogunwale. A million thanks to you.

Maggie Smith edited an earlier version of this manuscript, when I was trying to decide whether to keep writing or to give it up. I asked her afterward if she felt there was anything in my work to suggest that I should keep writing. Her response is the reason I persevered long enough for this book to emerge. Marjorie Oludhe Macgoye, the legendary Kenyan poet, in a March 4, 2010 letter sent in response to my earlier manuscript, said "Be blessed and illuminate your readers. I won't be around to see your coming volumes, but I wish you well and thank you for sharing your poems with me." I sincerely wished I could prove her wrong by having the book her guidance helped me write published in her lifetime, but I am 5 years too late. I will be eternally grateful to her, and to Professor Emilia Ilieva for introducing us. Kimiko Hahn advised me to "risk clarity." I know I have failed often at that in this book, Kimiko, but I will keep trying.

I gratefully acknowledge the editors and readers of the following publications, where earlier versions of some of the poems in this collection appear: *Humber Literary Review:* "1887: A Kidnap from Opobo"; *The American Journal of Poetry:* "Manubrium" and "Chaw"; *Under a Warm Green Linden*: "Sparus"; *Entropy*: "Grove"; *Canadian Medical Association Journal*: "Medical Séances"; *Black Bough Poetry*: "Child at Sleep"; *Obsidian: Literature & Arts in the African Diaspora*: "She Says—" and "We Will Have Questions" (nominated for the Pushcart Prize); *Pleiades*: "Tinderbox"; *Columbia Journal*: "Continental Want" and "Repair"; *SAND* Journal: "Gambit / Salvator"; and *Burning House Press*: "The Creation of Man" and "Via Negativa."

I owe a debt to the following poets, friends, and teachers who gave me much of my early literary education, and encouragement: Seyi Ogunyemi, Tosin Adeyemo, Toyin Olunloyo, Olatunde Asagba, Tade Ipadeola, Tolu Ogunlesi, Kola Oyekole, Ife Bamikole, Nyamachayi Chipawa, Segun Oluwatoke, Lateef Yusuff, Dami Ajayi, Wunmi Olabalu, Olumide Gbolahan, Seyi Alade, Segun Olorunda, Niran Okewole, Caitlyn Smith, Ms. Teboh, Mr. Iyiola, Mr. Alesin, Mrs. Ukpokolo, and Tosin Kolawole.

Thanks to the constellation that showed me my way: Donatus Nwoga, Wole Soyinka, Charles Simic, Esiaba Irobi, Yusef Komunyakaa, Warsan Shire, Femi Osofisan, Kola Onadipe, Ken Saro-Wiwa, Kofi Awoonor, Ben Okri, Mabel Segun, Ladan Osman, Mark Strand, Solmaz Sharif, Safia Elhillo, Kaveh Akbar, Natalie Diaz, Chris Abani, Danez Smith, Ada Limón, Victoria Chang, George Szirtes, Kamau Brathwaite, C.K. Williams, Safiya Sinclair, sam sax, Jumoke Verissimo, Gregory Pardlo, Raphael Armattoe, Terrance Hayes, Adrian Matejka, Carol Morrison, Kevin Young, Marcus Wicker, and J.P. Clark.

Profuse thanks to the Carnegie Library of Pittsburgh, Northland Public Library, the Allegheny County Library Association, Surrey Public Library, and Vancouver Public Library (shout out to the Public Library MFA) for the refuge and books I needed to read to write this one. For other resources that enabled me to complete this work, I am grateful for the Kenyon Review Writers Workshop; the literary companionship of Tiwaladeoluwa Adekunle, Esther Edoho, Adorah Nworah, Okaima Oyakhirome, and Tomilade Olugbemi; and the poetry prompts of Phillip B. Williams.

To my mother, who taught me to write; my grandfather, who sold books and taught me to love them; and to my father and siblings, I owe you more than I can say. To Caroline, Frances, and Zoe, my gratitude transcends language. This book is for you.

NOTES AND ATTRIBUTIONS

Note on the Cover Image: The cover image is a photograph of the Benin plaque "Warrior and Attendants," believed to have been created between the 16th and 17th centuries by the Edo people in what is now Nigeria. It is on view at The Metropolitan Museum of Art, having been gifted to it by Mr. and Mrs. Klaus G. Perls in 1990. Its provenance is given as "Court of Benin until 1897; (Sotheby's, London, May 20, 1964, no. 114); Paul Rose; Robert Owen Lehman, New York; Mr. and Mrs. Klaus G. Perls, New York, until 1990." Left unsaid was the sack of Ancient Benin by British forces in 1897, and the looting of palace treasures (including this piece) that subsequently made their way to auctions and collections around the world. https://www.metmuseum.org/art/collection/search/316393

Dan Hicks' book, *The Brutish Museums: The Benin Bronzes, Colonial Violence and Cultural Restitution* (published by Pluto Press in November 2020) explores this in more detail. I used the word "brutish" in the "1887: A Kidnap from Opobo" segment of the poem "A History of Treachery," in a way that is evidently similar to Hicks' title, but this similarity was a happy coincidence I only noticed between publication of *The Brutish Museums* and when this one went to press. I found it uncanny that we independently reached this insight about the colonial activities of the British, and thought to point out my awareness of this similarity.

"Lookout": "if we are indeed part of / a continent and not alone," is modified from John Donne's *Devotions* (1624):

"No man is an Island, entire of it self; every man is a piece of the Continent, a part of the main."

"Moose": draws from an article on DMV.org regarding wildlife collisions while driving.

"Medical Séances": the concept of séance as science is from Seyi Ogunyemi, reinforced by Terrance Hayes.

"AD79": is based on the story of the archeological find of the Vesuvius horse, preserved after the Pompeii eruption.

"In Which I, Again, am Fighting My Way Out of Things": "cheeto sun" was inspired by a line in the Danez Smith's poem "summer, somewhere," in their 2017 collection *Don't Call Us Dead.*

"Green / House": was written after C. K. Williams and incorporates, in sequence, the poem titles of C.K. Williams' final collection, *Falling Ill,* published in 2017. The poem titles are: "Flame," "Diagnosis," "Box," "Heading Home," "Pops," "My Body," "Telling," "Next," "Face," "First Dying," "Names," "You," "Tasks," "Really," "Eyes," "Bone," "Old," "Symptoms," "Secrets," "Labor," "Rays," "Better," "Rage," "Impatience," "My Double," "What," "Worse," "How Many," "Friends," "Fine," "The Past," "Everyone," "Here," "Coward," "Wounded Earth," "Embrace," "Bad Day," "The Heart," "Lonely," "Begun Again," "Can It Be Lost?," "Trees," "Crying," "Others," "Air," "Depression," "Day Off," "Against Me," "Lord Death," "Life," "Whenever," and "Farewell." The coin segment in section 1 was inspired by Aimee Nezhukumatathil's poem, "First Time in the Funicular."

"Our Lady of Delivery Excellence": "Call us / fardel" was inspired by the title of Tade Ipadeola's 2005 collection, *The Rain Fardel.*

"Repair": written after C. K. Williams and incorporates, in sequence, the titles of each of the 38 poems in C. K. Williams' 1999 collection of same title: "Ice," "The Train," "Archetypes," "After Auschwitz," "The Dress," "The Blow," "Bone," "Shock," "The Poet," "Stone," "Droplets," "Tender," "Risk," "House," "Naked," "Glass," "Shoe," "Dream," "The Cup," "Lost Wax," "Space," "Tantrum," "Not Soul," "Depths," "Tree," "King," "Owen: Seven Days," "Gas," "Last Things," "The Lie," "The Nail," "Canal," "The Dance," "Biopsy," "The Island," "Dirt," "Swifts," and "Invisible Mending."

"Sparus": is for Anthony Bourdain. "*Human bones / make for terrific daggers*" is from the title of an April 25, 2018 *Newsweek* article by Katherine Hignett concerning anthropological studies of New Guinea daggers.

"Life by a Thousand Bandages": is for Kola Oyekole, with thanks to Kevin Lysyk.

TOLU OLORUNTOBA is the author of the Anstruther Press chapbook *Manubrium*, shortlisted for the 2020 bpNichol Chapbook Award. His poetry has appeared or is forthcoming in *Harvard Divinity Bulletin, PRISM International, Columbia Journal, Obsidian,* and *Canadian Literature*, and has been nominated for the Pushcart Prize, while his short fiction has appeared in translation in *Dansk PEN Magazine*. He practiced medicine before his current work managing projects for health authorities in British Columbia. After a somewhat itinerant life in Nigeria and the United States, he emigrated to the Greater Vancouver Area, where he lives with his family in the territories of the Semiahmoo, Katzie, and Kwantlen First Nations.